BASKETS

by Nancy Schiffer

Historical Background by J.M. Adovasio

Schiffer Publishing Ltd

Box E, Exton, Pennsylvania 19341

The potting shed after a particularly windy snow storm.

Acknowledgments

We are indebted to many kind people who shared their knowledge, collections and enthusiasm toward the preparation of this book. Particular thanks go to S. Alexandride; Joan Alpert; Art and Kay Bransky; Jim and Donna Burk, Country Baskets, a partnership of Betty Berginski, Anita Metzbower, Sharon Schaeffer and Nancy Stump; Shirley and John Delph; Adele Earnest; Jeanie Eberhardt; Eugene and Dorothy Elgin; Vernon Gunnion; Gary and Dale Guyette; Harry Hartman; Lucile Henzke; Carroll Hopf; John E. McGuire; Dennis Moyer; Robert Neuman; Jane Niejadlik; Steven Rowe; Margaret Schiffer; Mr. and Mrs. Richard Flanders Smith; Martha Wetherbee; Robert and Pauline White. The *Historical Background* was edited by R.C. Carlisle, editor, Cultural Resource Management Program and typed by G. Lo Albo Placone, Department of Anthropology, University of Pittsburg.

Table of Contents

This book is dedicated to my parents who have always been there when I needed them.

Unique oak splint buttocks basket with hinged lid; Pennsylvania; 23 1/2" wide, 32 1/2" long, 11" high. (Pennsylvania Farm Museum)

A livingroom fireplace becomes the background for baskets used artistically as ornaments. Here, the floral arrangements are changed frequently to reflect seasonal and holiday themes. (Pauline White Collection)

An antique hat rack is used cleverly to display this group miniature splint baskets over a bucket bench with coil varieties. (From the collection of Jim and Donna Burk)

(John and Shirley Delph)

4

Living with Baskets

Baskets as useful objects long have served men in every aspect of daily life from the field to the table, from the garden to the market, and from the sewing room to the laundry. Modern homemakers who collect baskets are also using them decoratively both as objects on display and as useful forms other than for their original purposes. The following room settings are shown just as they were found in active, modern households. The enjoyment baskets give their owners every day in their homes is conveyed by their prominent and often numerous presence.

A large hamper basket has been inverted for use as a coffee table in this collector's living room. Part of a large basket collection is hung from a shelf and on the wall. Frequent changes and the addition of new acquisitions make this wall grouping a true study collection. (Pauline White Collection)

A fine variety of American Indian and traditional farm baskets fill this corner of a sitting room. (Harry Hartman, Marietta, Pennsylvania)

A basement work area remains functional while baskets and field tools decorate the walls. (Pauline White Collection)

In a warehouse converted to a home, baskets help to lower the ceiling height and add interesting focal points. On the right, dry tobacco leaves hang next to a tobacco leaf gathering basket stencilled by its owner from "Henderson, N.C.". (Harry Hartman, Marietta, Pennsylvania)

A hunting and fishing enthusiast has acquired an assortment of baskets and related sports objects. (Pauline White Collection)

The corner of an entrance hall contains a group of coil baskets of various forms and functions.

Coiled bee skep and large coil basket with handles used to decorate a painted cupboard in a modern home. (From the collection of Jim and Donna Burk)

A work space becomes the showplace of a collector's interests. (Joan Alpert Antiques)

This small pullman kitchen contains and is surrounded by useful baskets. (Harry Hartman, Marietta, Pennsylvania)

The corner of a collector's kitchen includes antique culinary tools and baskets (From the collection of Jim and Donna Burk)

Harry Hartman, Marietta, Pennsylvania.

The corner of a room at the Pennsylvania Farm
Museum of Landis Valley.

The center basket is lined with aluminum foil and used as a lampshade, being hung from a hook next to the electrical outlet. (Harry Hartman, Marietta, Pennsylvania)

Baskets are an integral part of this family room. (From the collection of Jim and Donna Burk)

The clever use of baskets hanging from a high ceiling adds texture and soft lines to this narrow but heavily used passageway.

Old and new baskets sit together where this basketmaker can study and compare. (Collection of Jane Niejadlik)

A corner of the diningroom where coil baskets are shown hanging on the wall and as useful containers. The chair seat is also made from woven splint. (Eugene and Dorothy Elgin)

The family room is a causual space in home with baskets used as decorative practical containers. (From the collectior Jim and Donna Burk)

This large tobacco leaf-drying basket dominates a corner of this sitting room with coiled baskets used as accents. (Harry Hartman, Marietta, Pennsylvania)

Coil openwork basket as it is displayed at the Pennsylvania Farm Museum.

Miniature baskets (see detail with dime for scale) give incredible reality to this small general store setting. (Pauline White Collection)

Coil openwork sewing basket on display at the Pennsylvania Farm Museum

New England baskets are kept on top of this Pennsylvania Kas. The unusual stave hamper was probably used to dry fruit. (Harry Hartman, Marietta, Pennsylvania)

A portion of the livingroom where a basket is used as an end table, and favorite baskets hold fruit and flowers. (Pauline White Collection)

Historical Background
J.M. Adovasio

Basketry is one of the oldest of mankind's crafts. In the New World, its antiquity extends back at least 11,000 years, and it is probably second in antiquity only to cordage and netting among the perishable fiber arts.

In the sense in which I use the term, basketry includes several distinct kinds of items. Rigid and semi-rigid containers (or baskets proper), matting and bags are all types of basketry. Matting is essentially two-dimensional or flat, and baskets are more clearly three-dimensional. Bags are intermediate forms in a sense because they are two-dimensional or flat when empty but three-dimensional when they are filled. As Driver (1961: 159) points out, all of these artifacts can be treated as a unit because the overall technique of manufacture is the same. Specifically, all forms of basketry are manually woven without frame or loom. Because all basketry is woven, it is technically a class or variety of textile although that term is sometimes restricted to cloth fabrics.

There are three major kinds or subclasses of basketry that are ordinarily mutually exclusive--twining, coiling and plaiting. Twining is a subclass of basket weaves made by passing moving (active) horizontal elements called wefts around stationary (passive) vertical elements called warps. Twining can be used to make containers, mats and bags as well as fishtraps, cradles, hats, clothing and other "atypical" basketry forms.

Coiling is a subclass of basket weaves in which stationary, horizontal elements (the foundation) are sewn with moving vertical elements (stitches). Coiling techniques are used almost exclusively to make containers and hats but very rarely bags. Mats and similar forms are seldom if ever produced by coiling.

Plaiting is a basket weave subclass in which all elements pass over and under each other without actual engagement. Technically, plaited basketry is therefore unsewn. Plaiting can be used to make containers, bags and mats as well as a wide range of other, less standard forms.

In commenting elsewhere on the preservation and distribution of basketry, I have noted (Adovasio 1977: 2) that:

Prehistoric basketry, in contrast to lithic or ceramic artifacts, is recovered intact only under special conditions. More or less stable environments, which are extremely dry, extremely cold or extremely wet, retard the decay and disintegration of basketry and other perishables by the exclusion of intermittent moisture, oxygen, bacteria or a combination of these agents of destruction. Basketry may also be preserved if it is in direct contact with the corrosion products of certain metals, notably copper, which act as bacteriacides. Thoroughly charred or incinerated specimens are insulated from further decay and may also be preserved for long periods if undisturbed.

Basketry remains from North America (and from most other parts of the world) have been found almost exclusively in dry caves and rockshelters. Occasionally, however, extensive assemblages of carbonized remains have been recovered from exposed sites in the Americas, Europe, Africa and Asia. Alaska, parts of Canada and Eurasia have yielded basketry in permafrost contexts. Waterlogged specimens have been encountered in North and middle America, as well as Europe, but this form of preservation is relatively rare.

The vast majority of prehistoric basketry has come from sites in the arid and semi-arid portions of western North America, including Mexico. Rockshelters and caves in Nevada, southern Oregon, Utah, Arizona, New Mexico, Colorado, western Texas, California, Arkansas and the Mexican states of Coahuila, Chihuahua, Tamaulipas, Puebla, Oaxaca, Durango, Michoacan and Guerrero have yielded tens of thousands of specimens, including many complete baskets, bags, mats and other kinds of objects. By comparison, the inventory from the remainder of the world is relatively meager. Collections from scattered locations in arid stretches of South America, the Nile Valley, the Near East and the Indian sub-continent rarely, if ever, approach the staggering mass obtained from the most productive North

American sites. Similarly, waterlogged, incinerated, metal-preserved or permafrozen assemblages from a thousand-odd localities across the planet do not equal in sheer numbers the assemblages from sites in the North American west.

The differential distribution of prehistoric basketry remains directly reflects not only conditions of preservation, but also the intensity of archaelogical research and the methods of excavation and recovery. In many parts of North America (notably, most of the southeast, midwest and northeast of the United States, as well as Canada), South America, Eurasia, Africa, Australia and Oceania, the only evidence survives in the form of impressions on pottery or on floors of buildings. Where even these clues are lacking, the student of prehistoric basketry must either focus on indirect evidence, such as the presence of awls or other specialized tools that may have been used in the production of basketry, or he must draw inferences from ethnographic and ethnohistoric information.

In short, the extant inventory of prehistoric basketry from all parts of the world is a dim reflection of the incidence of manufacture. Furthermore, only in very limited and geographically circumscribed areas can the sample that has been collected be considered representative.

Extensive studies of the prehistoric manufacture of perishables in western North America including Mexico conclusively indicate that the production of cordage (and presumably netting) was established in the western one-half of the continent by at least the 10th millennium B.C. The manufacture of basketry occurred only slightly thereafter. (See Adovasio, 1970a, 1970b, 1971, 1974, 1975a, 1975b, 1976, 1977, 1980a, 1980b, n.d. a, n.d. b, n.d. c, n.d. e; Adovasio and Andrews 1980, 1983, n.d.; Adovasio, Andrews and Carlisle 1976, 1977, n.d.; Adovasio, Andrews, Carlisle and Drennan n.d.; Adovasio, Carlisle and Andrews 1978; Adovasio and Gunn 1975, 1977; Adovasio et al. n.d.; Adovasio and Lynch 1973; Adovasio and Maslowski 1980; Andrews and Adovasio n.d.; Andrews, Adovasio, Carlisle, Frison and Edgar 1984).

Two receipt forms from English basketmakers: Henry Millett of Camomile Street, early nineteenth century; S. Middlebrook, Crispin Street, mid-nineteenth century. (Guildhall Library. City of London)

Historical Background

Significantly, the earliest basketry subclass recovered from *any* part of the arid American West with associated dates *prior* to the middle of the 8th millennium B.C. is twining. This occurs at the bottom of Fishbone Cave in western Nevada as early as 9250 B.C. (11,200 B.P.) and in such widely separated localities as Fort Rock Cave, Oregon (Cressman, et al. 1942; Bedwell 1973) and Danger Cave, Utah (Jennings 1957) at a time very near the end or just after the last Ice Age or Wisconsinan glaciation. Even by this relatively remote point in time, however, basketry was already so sophisticated in its execution that its antecedents must lie in the remote past. The same can be said for the quality of the earliest western cordage and netting.

Given these facts, I have suggested elsewhere (Adovasio, various) that cordage, netting, basketry and related fiber perishables may well have been part and parcel of the technological milieu of the first migrants to the New World. Confirmation of the presence let alone the roles that cordage, basketry and netting played in the technology of these "First Americans" may never be forthcoming, but data from western North America, Mesoamerica and South America lead us to believe that basketry and cordage production were established across the length and breadth of the New World by the 8th millennium B.C. at the latest (Adovasio and Lynch 1973; Adovasio and Maslowski 1980). Interestingly, the earliest Mesoamerican and South American basketry is also twined.

Recent studies of the much less substantial perishable data base from eastern North America seem to confirm the extreme age of basketry and related fiber industries (Adovasio and Andrews 1984). Indeed, several specimens from the vast area east of the Rockies *may* be the oldest dated examples of their kind on the planet.

These include a specimen of simple plaiting bracketed by radiocarbon dates of 10,850 + or − 870 B.C. and 9350 + or − 700 B.C. (12,800 + or − 870 and 11,300 + or − 700 B.P.) at Meadowcroft Rockshelter in Washington County, southwestern Pennsylvania (Stile 1982). There is an even older specimen of a cut, birch-like bark strip from near the bottom of the same site. This strip is directly dated at 17,650 + or − 2,400 B.C. (19,600 + or − 2,400 B.P.). It is not dissimilar in its overall appearance to the strips used in all of the subsequent Meadowcroft plaiting. *If* this specimen is indeed part of a plaited basket, it is not only the oldest known basket from eastern North America but, indeed, the oldest basketry now known in the world.

By the onset of essentially modern climatic conditions at ca. 8000 B.C. (ca. 10,000 B.P.), basketry and other perishables were represented in several parts of eastern North America (Adovasio and Andrews 1984). Like their contemporaries in the western United States, these are usually of twined construction. Representative sites for such basketry include Graham Cave, Missouri (Logan 1952; Klippel 1971) and Icehouse Bottom, Tennessee (Chapman and Adovasio 1977).

Twining seems to be virtually ubiquitous wherever basketry has been preserved from the remote past, but early plaiting, as noted above, is apparently restricted to eastern North America. Early coiling is even more limited in its distribution. It appears to have developed in a narrow belt or corridor extending from northern Utah through Arizona and down into arid northern Mexico. Invariably, the earliest coiled basketry takes the form of parching trays which are made on a single rod foundation (either whole or halved). The stitch is usually interlocking north of the Rio Grande and split on the non-work

Coil basket with bead decoration made as as gift by Pomo Indians of California. (Photograph courtesy Museum of the American Indian, Heye Foundation)

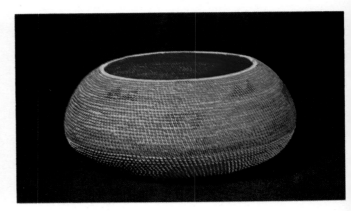

Coil basket decorated with feathers, made by William Benson, Pomo, California. (Photograph courtesy Museum of the American Indian, Heye Foundation)

surface (i.e., the basket surface from which the stitch emerges) in northern Mexico. (See Adovasio 1977 for definitions of these and other basketry terms.)

Whether invented once or repeatedly along this corridor, the origins of coiling seem to be inextricably connected to the specialized food preparation techniques used by desert-dwelling Archaic Indian populations. Seed parching requires parching trays, and these trays *cannot* be very successfully made by either twining or plaiting techniques. The surfaces of twined or plaited trays are susceptible to burning. In close coiling, however, with its tightly packed stitches, the probability of burning is reduced because the basket's surface allows a more even distribuition of heat (Adovasio 1970a: 22).

The archaeological record as it is now known also suggests that coiling never appears in an area, save in the case of cultural diffusion from another area, without the prior presence of a developed twining technology. Developmentally, it may be that coiling is the result of the elementary process of turning simple twining "sideways" and using one "warp" of indefinite length sewed back on itself rather than multiple warps of fixed lengths. Whatever the origin of coiling, once it had developed in the interior deserts, it spread rapidly to most parts of western North America where it became highly regionalized with a distinctive "local flavor." Coiling never penetrated to the east to any extent for reasons probably related to function.

By ca. 5000-4000 B.C. (ca. 6950-5950 B.P.), basketry was present virtually throughout North America, Mesoamerica and South America. By this time, regional basketry industries with varying technological characteristics and formal/functional attributes are distinguishable in the archaeological record (Adovasio 1974, 1980a).

Several millennia thereafer, around the beginning of the Christian Era or slightly before, basketry manufacture reached a prehistoric "apogee" of sorts in the American Southwest where highly distinctive coiling, fine twining (often in the form of flexible bags) and well-executed plaiting characterized the tripartite cultural complexes archaeologically known as Anasazi, Hohokam and Mogollon. Indeed, so common is basketry in the dry archaeological sites of Arizona, New Mexico and contiguous parts of Utah, Nevada, southern California and old Mexico that the Indian populations of these areas are sometimes called "Basketmaker," though that term is properly restricted to the early, pre-Pueblo Anasazi.

Although harder to document, concomitant

Southwest American Indian burden basket from 1920 or earlier. (Joan Alpert Antiques)

sophistication and diversity in basketry and textile manufacture is also seen during this same time period in eastern North America. Actual specimens, however, are rare, and most data are from impressions on pottery or clay (Adovasio and Andrews with Carlisle 1980). Despite the scarcity of the specimens themselves, however, it is certain that by the onset of the Woodland period, the technological foundations of perishable production had been firmly established all over the eastern half of the continent. This is evidenced in the manufacture of typologically diverse and technologically sophisticated forms that are *in no way inferior* to their better preserved counterparts in the arid West.

Sometime around A.D. 1200-1500 (750-450 B.P.), the broad outlines of what would become the basketry industries of ethnographic and ethnohistoric Indian groups were "in place" over all of the Americas where suitable plant raw materials were available and where alternative construction materials (e.g., leather, hide, fur, etc.) were not preferentially exploited. Space prohibits thorough discussion of the archaeological data from this period, but a few summary comments are warranted.

Half a millennium or so ago, the distribution of basketry techniques among American Indian populations mirrored rather closely both the

Islington Church in London with wicker-work steeple sheathing made by Thomas Birch, basketmaker, in 1787. (Guildhall Library. City of London)

Three basketmakers as published by W.H. Pyne, *Microcosm...*, vol. 2., 1804. (Guildhall Library. City of London)

immediately antecedent prehistoric perishable industries and their ethnographic progeny. Twining was the dominant or preferred technique on the Northwest Coast and in a restricted portion of Mexico. Both twining and coiling occured in Alaska, the Great Basin, the Southwest, the Plateau and most of California. In virtually all of these areas, twining occured sporadically on the Plains and in some sections of eastern North America, where it was ordinarily a minority technique.

Coiling dominated the basket making in virtually all of those areas where it is known to have co-existed with twining as well as in the Arctic, Subarctic, Baja California and certain parts of Mexico. Coiling was rare on the Plains, however, and was found only in the form of trays that ethnographically were used for a gambling game among certain Indian groups. Elsewhere in the East it is totally absent.

Plaiting was the principal basketry construction medium in eastern North America and most of Mexico. In other areas, notably the Plateau and the Northwest Coast, portions of the Plains and the Southwest, plaiting was a minority technique.

It is not feasible within the confines of this introduction to describe the archaeologically revealed genesis of specific ethnographic basketry making traditions or to discuss their salient characteristics, forms and functions. However, the character and diversity of ethnographic basketry is treated both in the remainder of this book and in other studies, most of which were produced years ago. The interested reader is advised to consult James (1903), Mason (1904), Weltfish (1930), the Denver Art Museum Leaflet Series and Lamb (1972) for further particulars. A complete list of basketry-producing North Ameri-

A basketmaker published by J. Luiken, Dutch, *Spiegel van het menselyk bedruyf*, 1767. (Guildhall Library. City of London)

A "Prickle Maker" published by T. Rowlandson. *Characteristic Sketches of the Lower Orders* in London in 1820. (Guildhall Library. City of London)

A basketmaker published in *The Book of English Trades*, anonymous, 1820, 1824, 1846 editions. (Guildhall Library. City of London)

Harry Hartman, Marietta, Pennsylvania.

can Indian tribes is available in Mason (1904) and Lamb (1972). Lists of plants used in basketry manufacture are to be found in Mason (1904) and in the Denver Art Museum Leaflet Series.

With the advent of European colonization and the subsequent percolation of Euro-Americans into all parts of the New World, the basketry industries of many, if not most Native American groups were rapidly altered, reduced or obliterated. Regretably, a craft that had flourished over the entire hemisphere for more than 11,100 years was effectively eradicated over much of its former range in less than three centuries. Whatever its remote origins, the end of most Native American basketry production had occurred by the turn of the present century. Although very fine work is still done here and there, and despite a resurgence of interest in the craft

among some present-day Indian groups (e.g., the Pima-Papago), the present range and scope, especially of North American basketry, is but a dim reflection of its prehistoric vigor and vibrancy. Strangely, it is in our own century that the individual regarded as the paramount American Indian basket maker, perhaps the greatest of all time, the Washo weaver, Dot-so-la-lee, flourished in Nevada. Her work, however, represents more the spectacular twilight of an essentially dying craft/art than a modern survival of it. However one views the genuinely magnificent fiber productions of this last and probably greatest of countless generations of nameless Indian basket makers, it is certain that collectively their work in this medium can be regarded as more characteristically and typically *American Indian* than any other artifact they ever produced.

24

A fine group of coiled and splint baskets. (Harry Hartman, Marietta, Pennsylvania)

L.L. Loud emerging from Lovelock Cave, Pershing County, Neveda with aboriginal decoys in a basket dating about 1,000 A.D. as found during excavations in 1924. (Photograph courtesy of Museum of the American Indian, Heye Foundation)

"The Young Merchants" oil painting by William Page about 1875. (Pennsylvaia Academy of the Fine Arts. Bequest of Henry C. Gibson)

"Buy a basket? large or small? For all sorts I've got by me." published by J.T. Smith. *The Cries of London*, 1839. (Guildhall Library. City of London)

New Jersey Pound Fishery at Monmouth Beach about 1935. (Peter J. Guthorn)

Makers, Tools and Materials

The people who made the baskets in this volume are rarely known; whenever possible, their names and locations are included. Baskets were generally utilitarian and not considered a product of pride to which the maker assigned his name. The rare signed examples are signposts to identify the style and materials used at a certain place and time.

Basketmakers used few specialized tools, if any. They cut their materials by hand or with a knife or axe. They prepared the materials with traditional hand-utilization methods and wove the baskets by hand. Occasionally wooden molds were made and woven over to form regular shapes. Willow rods were sometimes pulled through the cutting edges of a "brake" to peel the bark. Uniformly thick willow rods could be made by pulling wet shoots through holes in an iron bar.

The baskets in this volume are organized into three groups by the different materials used in their construction. The first group, and most numerous baskets, are made from wooden splints. A variety of wood types have been used, depending on local availability and customary preferences. The second group are made from reeds, often willow, and are known collectively as wicker baskets. The third are made of bundled straw coils that are then lashed together.

Baskets of European as well as native American heritage are found in splint weaves and coil construction, while wicker baskets were almost exclusively made by European weavers and their descendents. Grass weaving is found in native American cultures, and those examples are shown here among the splint baskets.

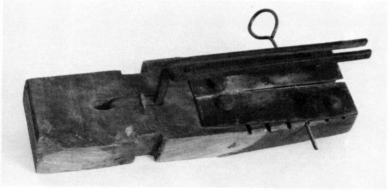

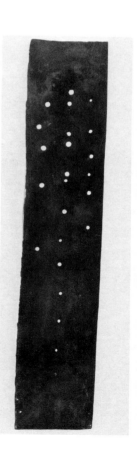

Both sides of a willow brake show the pin which is inserted at the converging blade edges to determine the width of the peeled willow rods.

The holes in this iron bar are graduated. Willow rods can be pulled through a hole to be shaved to a desired thickness.

This is a good example of an oak splint two-handled field basket made in the eastern United States about 1900. The splints are thick and strong with additional strengthening splints put along the bottom where the basket rests. A proud owner or maker has signed initials S.b.S. along one splint (Pauline White Collection)

Two oak stave field baskets. Left, factory-made with bentwood handles and stapled bands, 18" diameter, 11" high. Right, The owners' hand-crafted mourning dove decoys in a field basket with solid boards above and below the crossing staves at the bottom, and iron bail handle, factory made, 14 1/4" diameter, 9 1/2" high. (Robert and Pauline White)

Coil field basket with bentwood handles and wooden reinforcements protecting the bottom (see detail), from Chambersburg, Pennsylvania; 23" diameter, 10 1/2" high. (Eugene and Dorothy Elgin)

Two wicker market baskets; Southern European. Left, 8" wide, 4 1/4" deep, 6 1/2" high; Right, 8 1/2" wide, 5 7/8" deep, 7" high. (Pennsylvania Farm Museum)

A woman and a boy making baskets in 1929 at River Desert Algonkin area of Maniwaki, Quebec Province, Canada. (Photograph courtesy Museum of the American Indian, Heye Foundation)

Albra Lord, basketmaker seated and with his wife Sarah about 1925 in Lovell, Maine.

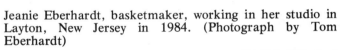
Jeanie Eberhardt, basketmaker, working in her studio in Layton, New Jersey in 1984. (Photograph by Tom Eberhardt)

Wicker laundry basket with two twisted handles and flat braided rim, 20" long, 13" high. (Pennsylvania Farm Museum)

Ash splint sewing baskets; Algonquin Indian; Maine; left, 9" diameter, 3" high; right, fitted with tools, 10 1/2" diameter, 3" high. (Joan Alpert Antiques)

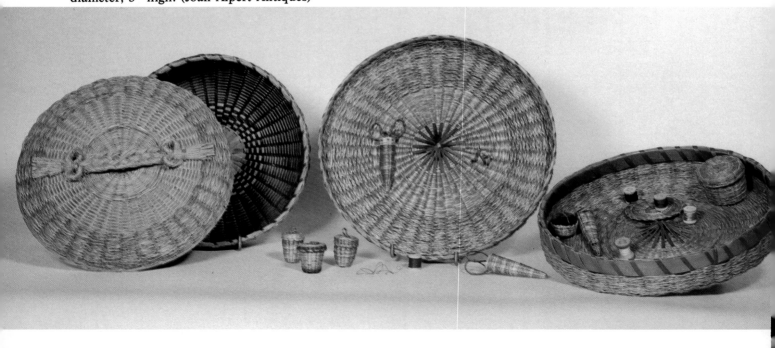

Splint Baskets

There will be seen in this volume a wide variety of basket types made from woven wood splint. The strong construction of splint weaving is suitable for field and burden baskets while thinner splint has been woven into every form of domestic work basket. Ash and oak splints were preferred in New England and the Mid-Atlantic regions respectively. Baskets made by New England Indians were frequently stamped with potatoe design decorations or splints were dyed with vegetable colorings.

The splint baskets have been arranged in groups to demonstrate covered, handleless, single-handle and double-handle types.

Ash splint sewing basket; Algonquin Indian; New England; 9" diameter. (From the Art and Kay Bransky Collection)

Natural reed sewing basket; by Sharon Shaeffer, Stevensville, Maryland; 1983. (Country Baskets)

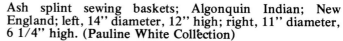

Ash splint sewing baskets; Algonquin Indian; New England; left, 14" diameter, 12" high; right, 11" diameter, 6 1/4" high. (Pauline White Collection)

Splint Baskets

Woven splint; Karok Indians, California. (Photograph courtesy Museum of the American Indian, Heye Foundation)

A very fine splint river cane basket made by Chitimacha Indians in Louisiana. (Photograph courtesy Museum of the American Indian, Heye Foundation)

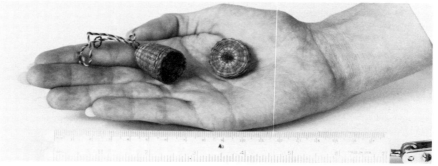

Dyed splint needle case; Chitimacha Indian; Louisiana. (Louisiana State University Museum of Geoscience)

Oak splint sewing basket; mid-Atlantic region.

Two covered splint baskets with purple dye. Made in 1875 by Wamanoag Indians in Massachusetts. Larger basket 7 3/4" long. (Photograph courtesy Museum of the American Indian. Heye Foundation)

Dyed splint miniature storage basket; Chitimacha Indian; Louisiana. (Louisiana State University Museum of Geoscience)

Oak splint sewing basket; New England.

Splint Baskets

Ash splint decorative baskets; New England Indian; left, with porcupine fancy weaving and wrapped, hinged handle, 12" diameter; right, with curly fancy weaving and two bentwood hinged handles.

Ash splint; Mic Mac Indian; Nova Scotia; 7" (Collection of Dale and Gary Guyette)

Splint 6-sided cheese basket with two side handles and lid handle; Pennsylvania; 10" diameter, 7 1/2" high. (Collection of Jim and Donna Burk)

Dyed ash splint handkerchief basket made for sale to tourists; Algonquin Indians in Maine; 8 1/2" square. (Joan Alpert Antique)

Ash splint feather basket with flat lid that slides up within the firm handle; New England; 8 1/4" diameter, 12" high. (Joan Alpert Antiques)

Close-up of the previous basket showing the unusual use of four wide ribs between the woven sides and the means of pinning the two lid flaps.

Small dyed splint storage basket; Chitimach Indian; Louisiana. (Louisiana State University of Geoscience)

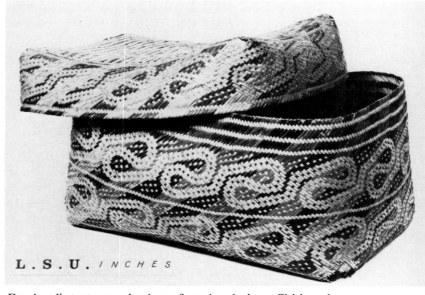

Dyed splint storage basket of snake design; Chitimacha Indian; Louisiana. (Louisiana State University of Geoscience)

Oak splint and round ribs storage basket; Pennsylvania.

Splint twill weave storage basket; Chitimacha Indian; Louisiana. (Louisiana State University Museum of Geoscience)

Tightly woven oak splint lunch basket or purse; Pennsylvania.

Dyed splint storage basket with stamped decoration; Onondaga Indian; New York. (Photograph courtesy Museum of the American Indian, Heye Foundation)

Two splint storage baskets traditionally recorded as holding goose feathers at plucking time; Pennsylvania; left, 10" wide, 20" high; right, 10" wide, 18" high. (Pennsylvania Farm Museum)

Dyed splint, large storage basket; Salish Indian; Canada. (Photograph courtesy Museum of the American Indian, Heye Foundation)

Modern brown ash lidded splint basket made by John E. McGuire of Hartford, Connecticut in 1983.

Left, rectangular ash splint picnic basket with two hinged handles and curly fancy weaving; Algonquin Indian; New England; 21" long, 8" high.

Right, round ash splint pie basket with sliding lid and firm handle, signed by an owner or maker "A. Shaughnessee" on handle, top, and three times on bottom; Pennsylvania; 12 1/2" diameter, 9" high.

Splint basket with remains of old green paint; Mic Mac Indian; Shelburne County, Nova Scotia; 8" diameter. (Collection of Dale and Gary Guyette)

Modern copy of a covered Nantucket Lightship style basket made by John E. McGuire of Hartford, Connecticut in 1983.

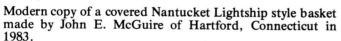

Oak splint lunch basket; Pennsylvania.

Oak splint lunch basket, factory made; Pennsylvania.

Poplar splint and willow lunch basket with double top flaps.

Three miniature purses; left and right, Chinese export rice
straw; center, splint by Shakers; New England.

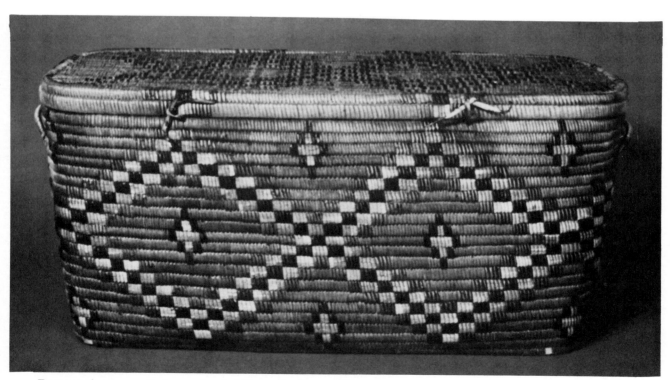

Rectangular covered storage basket from the Fraser River
of Canada. (Photograph courtesy Museum of the American
Indian, Heye Foundation)

Splint Baskets

Oak splint work basket with tin lining, perhaps for fishing; 7" wide, 7" high. (Pennsylvania Farm Museum)

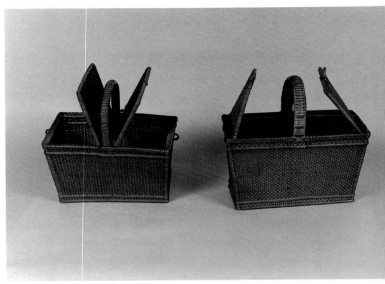

Two ash splint picnic baskets probably by Shakers; New England; left, 7" wide, 7" high; right, 8" wide, 7 1/2" high. (Pennsylvania Farm Museum)

Three rice straw containers; Chinese export; late nineteenth century; left, oval purse, 10" wide; center, bottle, 6 1/2" high; right, oval painted purse, handles missing, 11 1/2" wide.

Two rice straw baskets; Chinese expo[rt] left, handles missing and with pain[t] decoration, 8" long, 3 3/4" high; righ[t] 1/2" wide, 4 1/4" high with a croche[t] bottom which is probably a rep[lacement] (Schwenkfelder Museum)

Ash splint, probably by Shakers; New England; with a variety of weaving patterns and hinged wrapped handles, late nineteenth century, 11" long, 8 1/4" high.

Left, black ash splint fancy picnic hamper by the Shakers; New England; late nineteenth century, 13 1/2" long, 8" wide, 7 1/2" high. Right, thick poplar splint with two hinged handles. On the lid is a partial paper label reading "—SHVILLE—", 6 1/2" long, 9 1/2" wide, 7 1/2" high. (Robert and Pauline White)

Two ash splint picnic baskets probably by Shakers; New England, late nineteenth century; left, oval with firm wrapped handle, 10 1/4" long, 6 1/2" wide, 6 1/4" high; right, rectangular with hinged wrapped handles; 14" long, 8 1/4" wide, 8" high. (Schwenkfelder Museum)

Oak splint utility basket with black painted decoration, by Mohegan Indians in Connecticut, 10 3/4" long, 5 1/4" high. (Photograph courtesy Museum of the American Indian, Heye Foundation)

Dyed grass and splint utility basket made by Tlingit Indians, Sitka, Alaska. (Photograph courtesy Museum of the American Indian, Heye Foundation)

Dyed split cane utility basket; Cherokee Indians in North Carolina. (Photograph courtesy Museum of the American Indian, Heye Foundation)

Splint twill weave winnowing baskets by Chitimacha Indians in Louisiana. (Louisiana State University Museum of Geoscience)

Oak splint gathering basket branded on the side and base presumably by the maker, B.Beidman, Mid-Atlantic area.

Oak splint berry gathering basket and holder for five smaller ones; Pennsylvania.

Splint stave berry gathering baskets; two on left with iron rims and sawed openings in wide staves are of Shaker origin; New England. Center is a factory-made basket with solid wood bottom and staves tacked at the rims, 11" wide, 7 1/2" high; right, also tacked at the rim. (Pauline White Collection)

Splint flower gathering basket with a thin wash of grey paint inside; from Annapolis Valley, Nova Scotia; 24" long, 13 1/2" wide. (Collection of Dale and Gary Guyette)

Oak splint oyster gathering basket signed on the highest weaver by the maker Noah Newcomb, Dividing Creek, (New Jersey) 1940. The details show the high rising bottom to disperse the weight of the oysters to the sides of the basket, and the broad splints as they cross at the bottom. (Peter J. Guthorn)

Nest of three basket measures and 2 handled baskets, all made with oak splint ribs, cane weavers and reinforcements on the base. The measures are 8", 10" and 12" wide; the large handled basket 11" wide, 8" high. (Pauline White Collection)

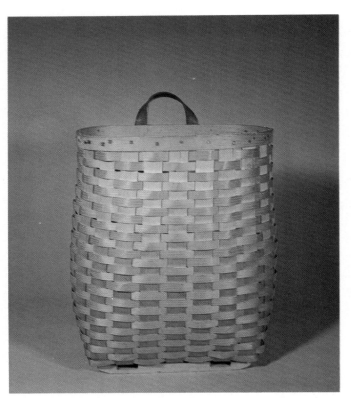

Splint hamper; Oriental; 14" diameter, 14" high the Art and Kay Bransky collection)

Oak splint back pack on reinforced base, with leather handle and nailed rim; 19 1/8" high, 15 1/8" wide, 11" deep.

Left, ash splint hamper 24" high, 13 1/2" diameter; right, oak splint market basket, Appalachian, 14 1/2" long, 9" deep, 15" high.

Dyed grass and splint utility basket made by Wishram Indians in Washington. (Photograph courtesy Museum of the American Indian, Heye Foundation)

Dyed twill-weave basket by Karok Indians in California. (Photograph courtesy Museum of the American Indian, Heye Foundation)

Splint carrying basket with a tumpline by Choctaw Indians in Mississippi. (Photograph courtesy Museum of the American Indian, Heye Foundation)

Woman with a pack basket, Eastern Cherokee Indian from North Carolina in 1904. (Photograph courtesy Museum of the American Indian, Heye Foundation)

Splint basket made by Gail Mau in 1983 after a Cherokee Indian design. (Natural Basketry. Photograph by Gerard Roy)

Dyed splint and stamped decoration; Algonquin Indians near Onondaga, New York. (Photograph courtesy Museum of the American Indian, Heye Foundation)

Unusual oak splint basket with uneven sides; Pennsylvania area; rim tacked, 13" wide, back: 9" high, front: 4" high. (Pennsylvania Farm Museum)

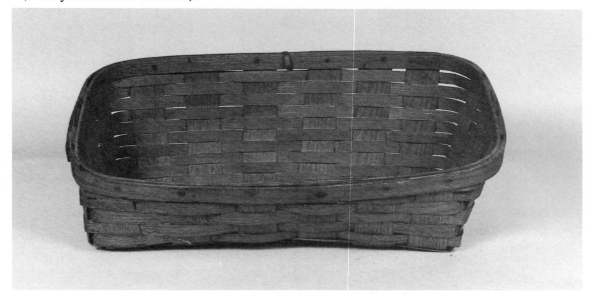

Thick oak splint rib-type corn gathering basket; probably Southern; 22 1/2" wide, 20" deep, 9" high. (Pauline White Collection)

Large field gathering basket from Pennsylvania with an oak splint raised foot. (Pennsylvania Farm Museum)

Oak splint gathering basket and miniature; Southern; 36" wide, 33" deep, 14" high.

Splint Baskets

Dyed splint utility basket fashioned after a Cherokee Indian design by Gail Mau, Branford, Connecticut, 1983. (Natural Basketry, Photograph by Gerard Roy)

Dyed splint and twine, rib-type basket.

Cane splint utility basket of interesting weave and light and dark splints; Oriental; 12'' diameter, 5 3/4'' high. (Pennsylvania Farm Museum)

(John and Shirley Delph)

Three varieties of oak splint baskets with different weaves; left, 8 1/2" diameter, 3 3/4" high; center, 9" diameter, 3 3/4" high; right, 9" diameter, 3 1/2" high. (Pennsylvania Farm Museum)

55

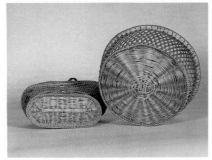

Group of four rice straw baskets, Oriental. The three on the left with painted decoration relate closely with the baskets on pages 43-45. The detail shows the same tight weave appearing on the bottoms of the large oval purse and the round utility basket with hexagonal weave. Leaft, miniature oval purse, 3 1/2" long, 2" deep, 3" high; oval purse 9 1/4" long, 5" deep, 4" high; miniature oval basket 3 1/4" long, right, round open work basket 10 3/4" diameter, 4 1/2" high.

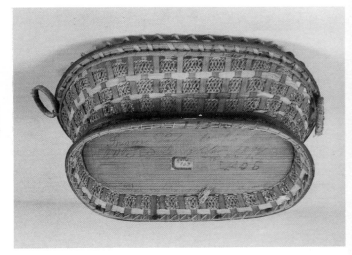

Fancy splint and woven sewing basket with solid wooden bottom inscribed "From Lizzie D. Allen to her daughter Rebecca E. Allen 1892. From Jafaris to his little daughter Lizzie D. Gray, 1898. 30 cents."

Oak splint on round ribs, pack basket, Pennsylvania, 27" wide, 14" high. (Pennsylvania Farm Museum)

Splint flat weave bread baskets; Southern, one is 7 1/4" wide the other is 8" wide, 3 1/4" high. (Pennsylvania Farm Museum)

Fancy splint and woven basket with silk lining and ribbon trim; Oriental; 8" long, 4 1/2" deep, 4 1/2" high. (Schwenkfelder Museum)

Splint Baskets

Oak splint seed sowing basket with two leather straps and side bentwood handles; New England; 15" wide, 10" deep, 7" high. (Joan Alpert Antiques)

Oak splint seed sowing basket with leather strap, canvas lining and wooden peg handle, Pennsylvania, 20" wide, 14" deep, 10" high.

Two oak splint seed sowing baskets from Cape Cod; left, with rope strap and peg handle, 14 1/2" long, 10 1/2" deep, 12" high; right, strap missing, 18" wide, 9 1/4" deep, 11" high. (Robert and Pauline White)

Dyed splint twill woven burden basket; Salish Indians of Canada. (Photograph courtesy Museum of the American Indian, Heye Foundation)

Twill-weave basket with geometric design made by Shasta Indians of California. (Photograph courtesy Museum of the American Indian, Heye Foundation)

Dyed grass and splint; by Wasco Indians in Oregon. (Photograph courtesy Museum of the American Indian, Heye Foundation)

Woven splint bonnet; English; early nineteenth century. (Herbert Schiffer Antiques)

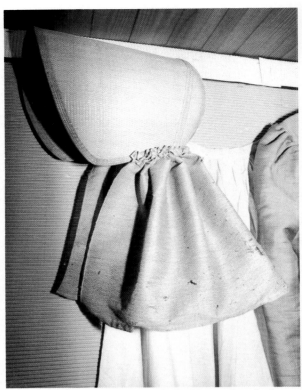

Woven splint bonnet; made in Pennsylvania by Quakers. (Schwenkfelder Museum)

Oak splint cat's bed with nailed rims; mid-Atlantic area; 19 1/2" wide, 15" high.

Oak splint eel trap with rope, wooden plug and orange buoy; South Carolina; 7 1/2" wide, 21" long. (Pauline White Collection)

Three ash splint baskets by Passamaquoddy Indians of Maine; Left, bobbin basket with dyed curly fancy decoration, 9" wide, 9 1/2" high; Center, round utility basket with porcupine fancy decoration, 7" diameter, 4" high; Right, bobbin basket with dyed curly fancy decoration 11 1/2" wide, 11 3/4" high. (Joan Alpert Antiques)

Splint Baskets

Red and green dyed ash splint strawberry whimsy with porcupine fancy woven decoration, Passamaquoddy Indians in Maine. (Joan Alpert Antiques)

Ash splint double tier bobbin basket, Mic Mac Indians of Shelborne County, Nova Scotia. (Collection of Dale and Gary Guyette)

Pennsylvania walnut antique furniture blends warmth and solidity, qualities further conveyed by the baskets which share space in this room.

Splint Baskets

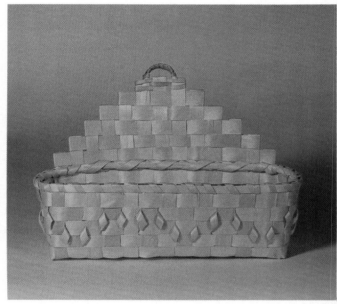

Ash splint bobbin basket, Mic Mac Indians, Maine.
(Pauline White Collection)

Ash splint bobbin basket with curly fancy decoration, Mic
Mac Indians, Maine, 10 1/4" long, 4" deep, 8" high.

Two ash splint bobbin baskets with differing weaves, Mic
Mac Indians of Maine.

Ash splint and sweet grass bobbin basket, Passamaquoddy Indians, Maine. (Joan Alpert Antiques)

Ash splint bobbin basket with curly and dyed splint decoration, and a miniature round basket attached, Passamaquoddy Indians, Maine.

Ash splint sewing basket with porcupine woven decoration; Passamaquoddy Indian, Maine.

Left top:
Oak splint cheese basket of hexagonal weave, detail shows wooden reinforcements on the base.

Left bottom:
Cheese basket attributed to the Mount Lebanon Shaker Community, late nineteenth century. (Collection of John E. McGuire)

Oak splint cradle, Appalachian, 40" long, 20" wide, 15" high.

Brown ash cradle on stand with fancy decoration; Passamaquoddy Indian; made by Mary Moore at Pleasant Point, Maine in 1950. (Joan Alpert Antiques)

Dyed twill woven baby carrier; made by Salish Indians Canada, 26" long, 9 1/2" wide. (Photograph court Museum of the American Indian, Heye Foundation)

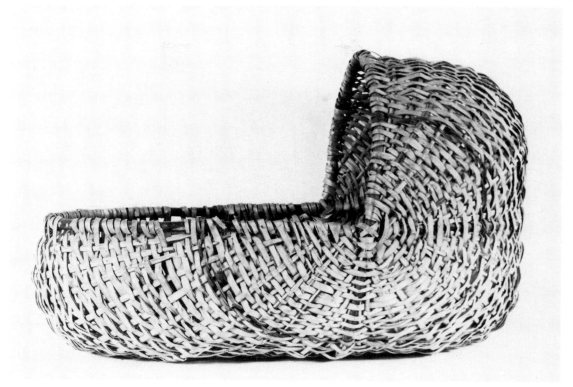

Oak splint cradle; probably made in Pennsylvania.

Large oak splint cradle, Southern.

(John and Shirley Delph)

Oak splint gathering basket known as a truge in its native England; 15 1/2" long, 8 1/2" wide, 9" high. (Robert and Pauline White)

Oak and pine splint painted basket made from a crate, marked on the bottom "W.H. Hogler, Hogestown, Pa. Aug. 17, MCMV" (1905), 22" long, 12 1/2" wide, 12" high. (Eugene and Dorothy Elgin)

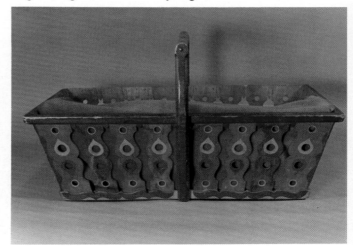

Three splint gathering baskets; left, 11" long, 9 1/2" high; right, small one, 9" diameter inside larger one, 15 1/2" diameter. (Pauline White Collection)

Three splint gathering baskets; left, oval, 15" long; center, rectangular, 26" long; front, Algonquin Indian, New England, with painted decoration, 6" long.

(John and Shirley Delph)

Eight oak splint baskets in a variety of forms including miniatures.

Oak splint baskets; left, market or egg basket, New England, on raised foot; right, gathering basket of rib construction, Appalachia.

Small oval oak splint gathering basket with wrapped handle.

Oak splint gathering basket, Pennsylvania.

Oak splint gathering basket probably for wood chips.

Seventeen miniature splint market baskets supported by an
antique towel rack.

Group of miniature baskets collected in northern New
England and representative of full-size baskets from that
area. Most of these are Indian-made and date from the last
half of the nineteenth century. The covered round basket at
the upper left, on the shelf is inscribed on the lid, "Indian
Encampment Saratoga Springs Aug. 1862". (Collection of
Steven Rowe)

Oak splint market basket and berry basket made by Mari D'onofrio, Branford, Connecticut, 1983. (Natural Basketry, Photograph by Gerard Roy)

Two oak splint egg or market baskets, left basket with footed base.

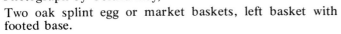

Unusual splint and round cane market or egg basket with openwork rim and footed base; Appalachian.

Oak splint market or egg basket with decorative wrapped band half way up the exterior side; Appalachian.

Three differing forms of miniature splint baskets from New England showing various handle attachments.

Left, oak splint herb gathering basket made to hang against a wall, 8 1/2" high; right, unusual splint basket with round ribs, cane and twisted handle, 5" diameter, 6 1/2" high. (Robert and Pauline White)

Red dyed splint and bamboo Easter basket; Oriental; 10" square, 12" high. (From the Art and Kay Bransky Collection)

Oak splint market basket with firm handle used in the laundry of the Pennsylvania Farm Museum at Landis Valley, Lancaster, Pennsylvania.

Five dyed splint and wicker Easter baskets, Oriental, left to right; twisted purple handle, 10'' long, 8'' wide, 11 1/2'' high; large red and gold, 12'' long, 18'' high; miniature with purple bow, 3 1/4'' diameter, 5 1/2'' high; two small baskets, 5 1/2'' long, 7'' high.

Left, splint miniature basket, 6'' diameter, 12'' high; Right, dyed woven splint and wicker Easter basket, 10'' diameter, 20'' high. (From the Art and Kay Bransky Collection)

Left, ash splint Easter basket on foot with wrapped handle, 12 1/2'' diameter, 19'' high; right, splint rib-style market basket on foot with bentwood handle, 12 1/2'' long, 9'' high.

Splint stave berry basket tacked at the rims, signed by an owner or maker "M.E. Purnell", probably New England.

Splint egg basket with stamped and red and black painted decoration; Mohegan Indian, Connecticut; 6 1/4" diameter, 7 1/4" high. (Photograph courtesy Museum of the American Indian, Heye Foundation)

Eight black ash or poplar splint baskets of various forms made by members of the Shaker community at Pittsfield, Massachusetts. (National Gallery of Art, Index of American Design)

Oak splint feather basket used at plucking time with firm handle, ribs tapered at both ends.

Splint Baskets

Splint hinged-handle market basket with square bottom found near New Ross, Nova Scotia, 10 1/2" diameter. (Collection of Dale and Gary Guyette)

Splint market basket with hinged handle, reinforced splint bottom and a thin grey wash of buttermilk paint, found in central Vermont; 12" diameter. (Collection of Dale and Gary Guyette)

Nest of four hinged-handle baskets made by Albra Lord of Lovell, Maine about 1925, sizes from 8 to 12" diameter. (Joan Alpert Antiques)

Splint Baskets

Left, oak splint berry basket with handle, New England, 3" diameter, 6" high; Right, berry basket with porcupine fancy weaving and woven ring handle, Algonquin Indian, New England, 2 1/2" diameter, 3 1/2" high.

Three miniature baskets and an American nickel coin to show scale; left, oval splint by New England Indians, 3" long; center, dyed splint with wrapped handle, 1 1/2" long, right, dyed coil with twisted twine handle. Southwest Indian, 3" diameter.

Eight Christmas tree ornaments in the forms of assorted fruit baskets with dyed raffia and splint holding artificial fruit.

Dyed splint market basket with wrapped handle, Chitimacha Indians, Louisiana. (Louisiana State University Museum of Geoscience)

Oak splint egg basket with wrapped handle, base and sides reinforced with extra oak ribs.

Dyed splint and wicker market basket with hinged handle, solid wooden bottom and tacked rim, mid-nineteenth century.

Splint and cane market basket with solid wood base and hinged handle, bearing paper label inscribed "Wm. D. Appleton, Nantucket, Mass.", c. 1910. 10" diameter. (Joan Alpert Antiques)

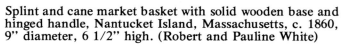

Splint and cane market basket with solid wooden base and hinged handle, Nantucket Island, Massachusetts, c. 1860, 9" diameter, 6 1/2" high. (Robert and Pauline White)

Dyed splint cane woven basket; Alibamu Indian, Texas. (Photograph courtesy Museum of the American Indian, Heye Foundation)

Splint cane twill woven market basket with wrapped handle; Choctaw Indians, Mississippi. (Photograph courtesy Museum of the American Indian, Heye Foundation)

Dyed ash splint market baskets with different hinged handle attachments; Algonquin Indian, New England; Left, 13 1/2" diameter, 10 1/2" high; Right, 12" diameter, 10" high. (Pauline White Collection)

Two rib-type baskets specialized to transport pigeons. Left, willow and reed; Right, oak splint.

Splint gathering basket made by Mari D'onofrio of Branford, Connecticut in 1983. (Natural Basketry, Photograph by Gerard Roy)

Oak splint factory made gathering basket with tacked rim.

Two oak splint gathering baskets. Left, with flat oak ribs; right, with round willow ribs. (Pennsylvania Farm Museum)

Two chestnut splint baskets made by Luca Bova in Tremonti, Italy in 1980. Larger, 18" long, 13" wide, 16 1/2" high. Joan Alpert Antiques.

(John and Shirley Delph)

Tin basket copied from an old original by David Claggett, Christiana, Pennsylvania, 1984; 8 1/4" long, 8" high.

Group of Shaker-made containers. Left, yellow painted maple basket with oak handle and pine bottom; Hancock Shaker Community, Massachusetts; 14 1/2" long, 11 1/2" wide, 10" high; Center, nest of four wild cherry boxes, Sabbathday Lake Shaker Community, Maine. Right, half-bushel measure marked "United Society. W. Glouces-ter, Me.", c. 1870, 14 3/4" diameter, 8" high. (Joan Alpert Antiques)

Splint flower gathering basket made by Joe Knockwood, a Mic Mac Indian in the Strong-Farmington area of Maine in the 1920's. Joe Knockwood stamped his baskets with his trade-mark of an Indian in head dress and the name Knockwood. (see bottom of basket) 20" long, 10" wide, 4" high. (Joan Alpert Antiques)

91

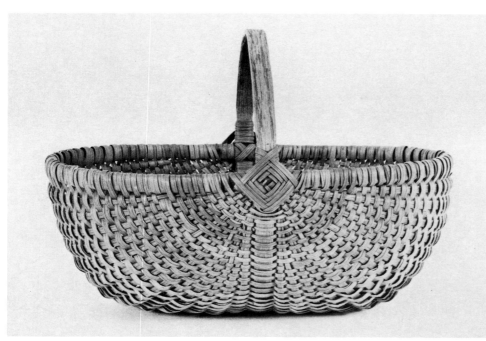

Five assorted miniature oak splint rib-type baskets with different "God's eye" crossing splint handle supports.

Rib-type white oak market basket with firm handle and "God's eye" crossing splint handle supports.

Oak splint rib-type buttocks basket with firm handle and "God's eye" crossing splint supports.

Three splint rib-type market baskets; Southern.

Two oak splint rib-type baskets with inter-woven central ribs and different "God's eye" crossing splint handle supports; Appalachian area.

Splint rib-type potatoe picking basket designed so that the basket could be dunked into water to wash the potatoes, 16 1/2" long, 14 1/2" wide, 13 1/2" high.

Four miniature splint baskets. Left, New England Indian sewing tool basket for a sewing basket, 3" long, 1" high; left of center, very small buttocks style 2 1/2" wide, 2" high; right, round rib-type form also called an "Armadillo" with painted surface; Front, miniature buttocks one-egg basket. (Pauline White Collection)

Oak splint market basket with tapering ribs, used here to hold shore-bird decoys. (Adele Earnest)

Three dyed splint baskets. Left, "Oriole" nest-shaped basket purse 8 1/2" wide, 5 1/2" deep, 15" high; center, miniature rib-type "melon" basket, 3" diameter; right, round market basket on raised foot, 9" diameter.

ak splint egg basket on wrapped, raised foot; ' high.

Melon basket with bittersweet vines and sea grass made by Mari D'Onofrio, Branford, Connecticut. (Natural Basketry. Photograph by Gerard Roy)

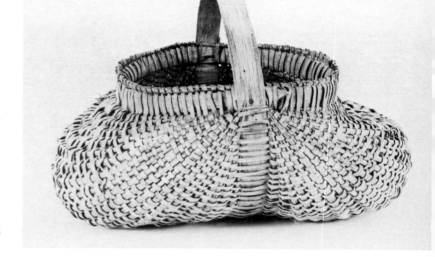

Oak splint rib-type buttocks basket with firm handle tacked to the rim; Appalachia.

Rib-type splint buttocks basket with twisted handle.

Rib-type splint basket called a "baby carrier" with twisted handle; 24 1/2" long, 16" wide, 16" high. (Joan Alpert Antiques)

Rib-type splint market basket and miniature, each of deep oval form with twisted handles; larger; 20" long; smaller, 6 1/2" long.

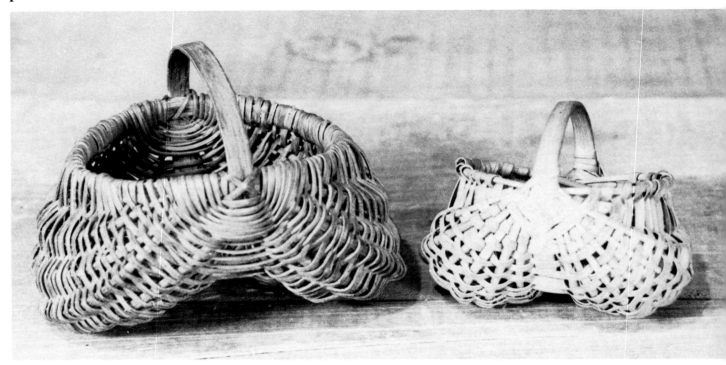

Two miniature oak splint rib-type buttocks baskets with
firm handles; Appalachia.

Two vegetable baskets of factory make with nailed rims.
Left, 7 1/2" long, 5" high. Right, 10" long, 6" high.
(Pennsylvania Farm Museum)

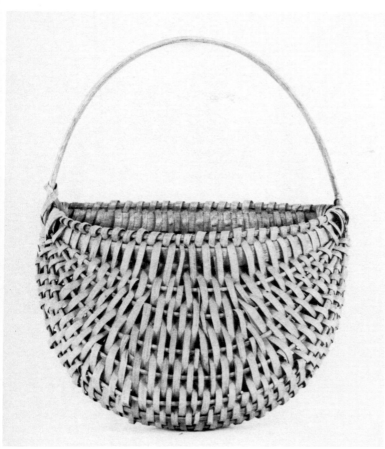

Splint rib-type "oriole" nest-shaped basket with oak handle and rim, round reed ribs; Southern.

Dyed red rib-type buttocks egg basket made by Sharon Schaeffer of Stevensville, Maryland in 1983; 14" wide. (Country Baskets)

Modern dyed splint and reed buttocks basket with God's eye attachment for the wrapped handle. (Natural Basketry. Photograph by Gerard Roy)

White oak splint market basket made by Nancy Rose at the Museum of Southern Appalachia, Norris, Tennessee, in 1983; 9 1/2" long, 6 1/2" wide, 10" high.

Rib-type buttocks basket with green painted rim and handle; New England; mid-nineteenth century; 14" long, 10" wide, 9" high. (Joan Alpert Antiques)

Reed and splint rib-type hen basket made by Anita
Metzhower in 1983; 14" wide. (Country Baskets)

Three oak splint rib-type buttocks baskets; Southern;
Miniature, 3" diameter; half-basket, 9" wide; Large, 24"
diameter.

Melon basket made by Tara Cullaghan, Branford, Connecticut. (Natural Basketry, Photograph by Gerard Roy)

Basket woven by Mari D'Onofrio, Branford, Connecticut. (Natural Basketry, photograph by Gerard Roy)

Contemporary melon basket made by John McGuire. Hartford, Connecticut.

Double melon basket woven by Keith Hatcher. (Collection of Mari D'Onofrio. Natural Basketry. Photograph by Gerard Roy)

Melon basket with twig handle made by Mari D'Onofrio, Branford, Connecticut, 1983. (Natural Basketry, Photograph by Gerard Roy)

Two oak splint rib-type half baskets. Left, with arched back and dyed splints from Westminster, Maryland; 6" wide, 3 1/2" deep, 8" high. Right, with old silk cloth backing from Winchester, Virginia; 7" wide, 5" deep, 12 1/2" high. (Eugene and Dorothy Elgin)

Three splint half baskets; Left, wide oak woven splint with tacked rim, 8" wide; Center, rib-type oak splint buttocks style, 12" wide; Right, painted rib type buttocks style, 10 1/2" wide.

Left, unusual oak splint purse with interlocking frame ribs. Right, oak splint rib-type "Oriole" nest-shaped purse.

Baskets made from pine cone scales by Rappahannock Indians at Indian Neck. King and Queen County, Virginia. (Photograph courtesy Museum of the American Indian, Heye Foundation)

Man shown dipping fish into a fish basket within this trap in 1923. Arikara Indian at Fort Berthold Reservation in North Dakota. (Photograph courtesy of Museum of the American Indian, Heye Foundation)

Splint Baskets

Oak splint hanging basket by Choctaw Indians in Mississippi. (Photograph courtesy Museum of the American Indian, Heye Foundation)

Very unusual sweet grass pitcher, Northern Maine; 9" high. (Collection of Dale and Gary Guyette)

Heavy splint field basket with the remains of grey-green paint inside and out and a solid wooden bottom; 22 1/2" diameter, 21 3/4" high.

Left, oak splint and cane weaving field basket with tin strap reinforcements crossing at the bottom with iron pin, rope handles, 18 1/2" diameter, 13 1/2" high; right, oak splint field basket with hand grips at top rim, bottom branded "OHND UDE Y", 15 1/2" diameter, 12" high. (Robert and Pauline White)

Oak splint field basket with tacked rim.

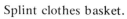

Splint clothes basket.

Oak splint clothes basket; New England.

Splint clothes basket with tacked rim and solid bottom. The handles may not be original. Rim marked in black crayon "39 cents".

Ash splint basket and bottom detail, probably made by an Indian group in New England.

Reproduction of a New England oak splint field basket made in 1983 by Mari D'Onofrio. (Natural Basketry, Photograph by Gerard Roy)

Left, ash splint field basket made at Dantown (Stamford), Connecticut circa 1875, 15" diameter, 12" high; right, double pie basket with wire hinges made by members of the Shaker Community at Enfield, New Hampshire, handles marked "HH", 18 1/4" long, 10" wide, 5" high. (Joan Alpert Antiques)

Two iron wire and oak rimmed baskets for gathering clams;
Southern New Jersey; left, 18" wide, 13" high; right, 13
3/4" wide, 7 1/2" high. (Pauline White Collection)

Ash splint pie basket with two hinged handles; New
England.

Splint coal winnowing basket from Maine. By shaking, the large coal chunks for fuel could be separated from the coal dust which was collected and used to make medicines, 37" wide, 28" high. (Joan Alpert Antiques)

Red and green dyed ash splint fruit drying basket made by Penobscot Indians in Maine about 1920; 20 1/4" long, 14 1/2" wide, 5" high. (Joan Alpert Antiques)

Splint fruit drying basket; 24 1/2" long, 22" wide, 6" hig (Robert and Pauline White)

Two splint field baskets with side handles; top, 40" long,
24" wide; bottom, 22 1/2" square. (Harry Hartman,
Marietta, Pennsylvania)

Splint Baskets

Brown ash splint field basket made about 1925 by Albra Lord from Lovell, Maine. 19" diameter, 12" high. (Collection of Sally Davey)

Oak splint wool drying basket on four legs.

:h splint sewing basket with curly fancy weaving and eight xagonal-weave small baskets for tools attached to the n. Made by Algonquin Indians and used by members of a :w England Shaker Community. (Joan Alpert Antiques)

Splint wool drying basket on four legs with thick bottom reinforcements; New England; late nineteenth century, 24 1/2" wide, 14" high. (Joan Alpert Antiques)

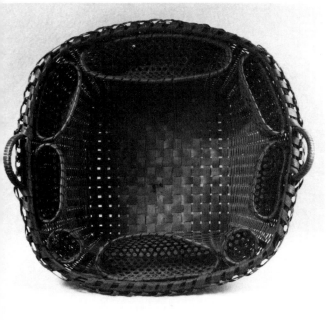

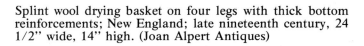

Splint copy of a field basket by Mari D'onofrio of Branford, Connecticut; 1983. (Natural Basketry, Photograph by Gerard Roy)

Twisted sea grass "Potatoe basket" by Mari D'Onofrio, Brandord, Connecticut. (Natural Basketry, photograph by Gerard Roy)

Page 118. The diningroom cupboard is surrounded by a casual display of baskets. (Pauline White Collection)

Page 119. In a small laundry - powderroom, baskets are used for various practical uses. (Harry Hartman, Marietta, Pennsylvania)

Left, white ash splint and reed double pie basket made by Nancy Stump of Stevensville, Maryland, 1983; Center, splint and reed potatoe basket made by Betty Berginski, Stevensville, Maryland. 22" long, 18" wide; right, splint and reed double apple basket, made by Betty Berginski, Stevensville, Maryland, 8" diameter. (Country Baskets)

Left, below, a market basket made in 1983 by John McGuuire, Hartford, Connecticut.

Harry Hartman, Marietta, Pennsylvania

Modern covered basket on four feet made in 1983 by John McGuire, Hartford, Connecticut.

Wicker Baskets

Three wicker market baskets of Southern European origin. Left, 14" wide, 8 1/2" deep, 14 1/2" high; center, 12" wide, 9" deep, 7 1/2" high; right, 17" wide, 9 3/4" deep, 11" high. (Pennsylvania Farm Museum)

Two wicker market baskets; Left, 12" wide, 10" deep, 7" high; Right, straw and cane weave, Oriental, 10" wide, 6" deep, 8" high. (Pauline White Collection)

Most wicker baskets have been made from willow reeds according to European weaving traditions. The shapes are frequently of European extraction, and those made in the United States are usually from regions settled by European immigrants. These examples include unpeeled (dark) and peeled (light) willow reeds, and some have been colored before or after weaving. The variety of wicker forms is vast. These examples are arranged in groups of covered, handleless, single handle and double handle types.

Wicker picnic basket; Pennsylvania; 26'' wide, 16'' deep, 12'' high. (Pennsylvania Farm Museum)

Wicker market basket with a variety of weaves, 13'' wide, 11'' high.

Left, dyed wicker market basket, 16'' wide, 9'' deep, 10 1/2'' high. (Herbert Schiffer Antiques); right, wicker hamper, 15'' wide, 13'' deep, 6 1/2'' high. (Ellen J. Taylor)

Wicker Baskets

Dyed wicker hamper from Pennsylvania; 18" wide, 11 1/2" deep, 8 1/2" high. (Pennsylvania Farm Museum)

Wicker picnic basket marked "Coracle, Made in England". c. 1950, 22" wide, 13" deep, 7 1/2" high.

Wicker clothes hamper; Pennsylvania; 22 1/2" square, 30" high. (Pennsylvania Farm Museum)

Left, large painted wicker hamper 18" diameter, 17 1/2" high; right, wicker bird cage, 19" high. (Pennsylvania Farm Museum)

Wicker pet carrier, 17" high. (Pennsylvania Farm Museum)

Wicker doll's carriage, c. 1915. 20" wide, 21" high. (From the Art and Kay Bransky Collection)

Hot air ballooning basket, 1983. 48" long, 72" wide, 53" high. (Raven Industries, Inc.)

Modern ballooning basket made by The Balloon Works.

A Stairwell became the fishing closet. (Pauline White Collection)

Two wicker fishing creels; left, with leather strap reinforcements, 14" wide, 8" high; right, with woven strap, 12" wide, 7" high. (Pauline White Collection)

Rush wicker baskets made by Rappahannock Indians at Indian Neck, King and Queen County, Virginia. (Photograph courtesy Museum of the American Indian, Heye Foundation)

Two honeysuckle wicker baskets made by Mattapony Indians at the Mattapony Reservation at King William County, Virginia. (Photograph courtesy Museum of the American Indian, Heye Foundation)

Baskets at an outdoor market in India. (Photograph by Norman Kranzdorf)

Two wicker trays, Pennsylvania; left, oval with two ha[ndles], 18" long, 14" wide, 2 1/2" high; right, rectangular[...] long, 14" wide, 5 1/2" high. (Pennsylvania Farm Mu[seum])

Two wicker bread baskets; left, made from the rushes of the River Shannon in Ireland, 8" diameter, 4" high; right, made by John Crane of County Mayo, Ireland, circa 1930, 14" diameter, 7" high. (From the Art and Kay Bransky Collection)

Two wicker trays; Pennsylvania; round, 15" diameter, 3" high; rectangular with solid wooden bottom, 19" long, 11" wide, 4" high. (Pennsylvania Farm Museum)

Wicker Baskets

Cane and splint utility basket.

Wicker and braided reed utility basket.

Wicker bread basket, 10 1/2" long, 5 1/2" high.
(Pennsylvania Farm Museum)

Triple woven basket by Mari D'Onofrio, Branford, Connecticut. (Natural Basketry, Photograph by Gerard Roy)

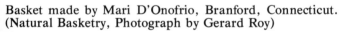

Basket made by Mari D'Onofrio, Branford, Connecticut. (Natural Basketry, Photograph by Gerard Roy)

Black basket with spiral design by Mari D'Onofrio, Branford, Connecticut. (Natural Basketry. Photograph by Gerard Roy)

Wicker Baskets

Red triple woven basket made by Mari D'Onofrio, Branford, Connecticut in 1983. (Natural Basketry, Photograph by Gerard Roy)

Blue triple woven basket made by Mari D'Onofrio, Branford, Connecticut in 1983. (Natural Basketry, Photograph by Gerard Roy)

Left, wicker covered clear glass bottle with cork stopper, 5" wide, 10" high; right, wicker vase 6 1/4" high. (Robert and Pauline White)

Wicker gathering basket with solid wooden bottom, 20" long, 17 1/2" wide, 8 1/2" high. (Pennsylvania Farm Museum)

Wicker gathering basket with wicker bottom, 18" long, 12" wide, 9" high. (Pennsylvania Farm Museum)

Wicker and braided straw fruit basket with solid wooden bottom stamped "Charles & Co., grocers, and fruiterers, New York." late nineteenth century, 12" long, 8 1/2" deep, 14" high. (Robert and Pauline White)

Wicker Baskets

Wicker market basket with lid for transporting small birds and animals, New England, nineteenth century. (Joan Alpert Antiques)

Two wicker market baskets, Appalachian.

Wicker market basket with oak handle, Pennsylvania.

Two wicker baskets; left, large round; right, market basket with twisted handle.

Wicker market basket with twisted handle.

Three wicker kitchen baskets; Left, cornucopia, modern, 13 1/2" long, 8 1/2" diameter; Center, bread basket, 9" diameter, 3 1/2" high; Right, market basket 9 1/4" diameter, 9" high.

Two fancy wicker sewing baskets; left, with pink ribbon trim, 8 1/2" diameter, 4 1/2" high; right, with twisted wicker handle, 9" diameter, 5 1/2" high. (Pennsylvania Farm Museum)

Three wicker farm baskets; left, round market basket with twisted handle, 12" diameter, 9" high; center, round laundry basket with two twisted handles, 16 1/2" diameter, 10 1/2" high; right, oval market basket with wrapped handle; 11" long, 9" wide, 7 1/2" high. (Pennsylvania Farm Museum)

Two wicker market baskets; left, oval with green painted flat woven rim and twisted handle, 12" long, 9" deep, 5" high; right, red painted basket with wrapped handle, 6" diameter, 8" high. (Pennsylvania Farm Museum)

Two wicker fancy openwork baskets; left, painted wicker and splint flower vase with wicker handle, 12" high; right, round bread basket with two ring handles, 7" diameter, 5" high. (From the Art and Kay Bransky Collection)

Bundled twigs joined to form a basket which accompanied a Negro doll called "Moses in the Basket", German, 1897. 14" long, 11" high. (From the Art and Kay Bransky Collection)

Wicker laundry or field basket with twisted handle, 17" diameter, 13 1/2" high. (Pennsylvania Farm Museum)

Two wicker baskets; left, hen market basket; right, covered utility or sewing basket.

Wicker laundry or field basket with twisted handle.

Wicker market basket with twisted handle. (Pennsylvania Farm Museum)

A two-handled laundry wicker basket and five graduated
egg or market baskets, all from Southeastern Pennsylvania.

Two small utility baskets with twisted handles.

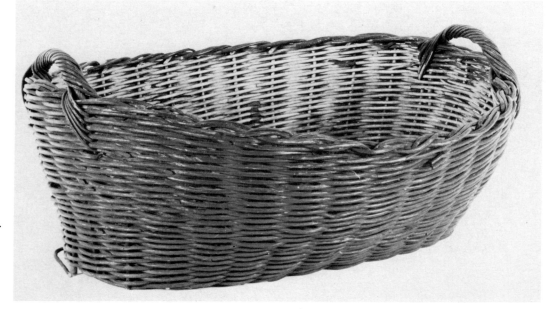

Painted oval wicker laundry basket with two twisted handles.

Wicker flower basket with two twisted handles, 10" diameter, 10" high. (Pennsylvania Farm Museum)

Tall wicker hamper with two twisted handles, 16" diameter, 28" high. (Pennsylvania Farm Museum)

Two fancy English Wicker and braided raffia baskets; left, egg shaped purse or holder for glass Easter egg, 7" long, 4 1/2" high; right, four-footed cane and fancy woven basket, 6" diameter, 3 3/4" high. (Pauline White Collection)

Coil Baskets

Bundled straw coils have been used to make baskets for thousands of years (See *Historical Background*) in a wide variety of forms. American Indian traditions include coiled baskets for work-related and ceremonial uses. The Pennsylvania German immigrants have frequently used rye straw coils to form their utilitarian baskets lashing them together in a variety of styles including attractive openwork. This selection of coil baskets are arranged in groups representing covered, handleless, single handle and double handle types.

Coiled basket and cover made by Chumash Indians in California. (Photograph courtesy Museum of the Indians, Heye Foundation)

Coiled covered basket with two bentwood handles; 15 1/2" long, 10" deep, 7" high.

Coil covered basket probably used for sewing, with bentwood handles made by a basketmaker from Ephrata, Pennsylvania.

Covered coil basket with the remains of two handle attachments seen at the bottom of the basket. These seem to resemble the work of a basketmaker from Ephrata, Pennsylvania. Other examples of his work follow.

Covered rye coil baskets at home in the kitchen.

Two covered coil baskets from Tonytown, Maryland; the shorter one 16 1/2" wide, 9 1/2" high. (Eugene and Dorothy Elgin)

Coil Baskets

A covered coil basket of unusual bulbous form has oak splint weavers. Made in New Oxford, Pennsylvania, 16" diameter, 22" high. (Eugene and Dorothy Elgin)

Covered rye coil baskets used with antique country furniture in a modern home. (From the collection of Donna and Jim Burk)

Two large storage baskets from central Pennsylvania. (Eugene and Dorothy Elgin)

The space under the stairs becomes an interesting view with this foreign, covered, coil, storage basket.

Coil Baskets

Covered coil basket of unusual footed form, 18" diameter, 13" high. (From the collection of Jim and Donna Burk)

Large covered coil basket from Gettysburg, Pennsylvania; 27" wide, 21" high. (Eugene and Dorothy Elgin)

This is a great hiding place.

A covered rye coil basket accents country furniture in the living quarters. (Harry Hartman, Marietta, Pennsylvania)

Large covered coil basket with bentwood handles carved in a characteristic manner (see detail) by a basketmaker from Ephrata, Pennsylvania. 33" long, 25" deep, 14 1/2" high. (Eugene and Dorothy Elgin)

Large coil storage basket woven with twine and with 2 side handles, from Scotland.

Chinese coil and splint tea pot cozy with 2 cups and saucers and 2 spoons inside, lined and padded with red silk; 12" long, 9" deep, 8" high.

Nest of 3 coil baskets woven with feather decoration on the lids. Smallest, 4 1/2" diameter; largest, 9 3/4" diameter.

Long covered coil basket with leather looped hinges; 24" long, 11" wide, 7" high. (From the collection of Jim and Donna Burk)

Two covered coil openwork baskets; Left, rectangular picnic basket with two hinged handles; 16" long, 8" wide, 8 1/4" high; right, oval coil openwork basket and cover, 5" wide, 6" high.

Two covered coil baskets with whale designs made by Makah Indians in Washington state. (Photograph courtesy Museum of the American Indian, Heye Foundation)

Left, oval coil basket with lid and braided handle; 14 1/2" long, 9" high. Right, Chinese square coil basket with painted cane decoration, 8 1/2" square, 3" high. (Pauline White Collection)

Coiled covered basket of yarn around paper core made by Jeanie Eberhardt of Layton, New Jersey, 1983. (Photograph, Richard Brown & Assoc.)

Modern covered coil basket with colored decorations made in 1983 by Jane Niejadlik, Northampton, Massachusetts.

Round coil storage basket with two flaring rows of rim coils, made in Irishtown, Pennsylvania, 12" wide, 11 1/2" high. (Eugene and Dorothy Elgin)

The livingroom corner cupboard contains a collection of baskets. (From the collection of of Jim and Donna Burk)

Coil and splint baskets are used as decorative features in this diningroom. (From the collection of Jim and Donna Burk)

Coil measure hollow at both ends, 10 1/2" diameter, 16" high overall, open 10" from one end and 6" from the other.

Coil basket of dyed grass, bark, and roots woven tightly to hold water; Northwest Indian; 7" diameter, 9 1/2" high. (Joan Alpert Antiques)

Two coil baskets; left, made by Hopi Indians in New Mexico or Arizona, 9 1/8" diameter; right, from Oklahoma, 10 3/4" long, 9 1/4" wide.

Dished coil basket made by the Topato Indians in Northwest United States; 17 3/4" diameter. (Eugene and Dorothy Elgin)

Dyed coil bottle neck basket made by Yokuts Indians of California. (Photograph courtesy Museum of the American Indian, Heye Foundation)

Coil bottle-necked basket made by Mono Indians in California. (Photograph courtesy Museum of the American Indian, Heye Foundation)

Coil Baskets

Coil basket with Pookang design made by the Hopi Indians of Arizona.

Large coil canoe-shaped basket with solid feather decoration made by Pomo Indians in California. (Photograph courtesy Museum of the American Indian, Heye Foundation)

Coil and grapevine basket made by Jeanie Eberhardt, of
Layton, New Jersey in 1983. 8 1/2" diameter, 6" high.
(Photograph, Richard Brown & Assoc.)

Coil and woven basket made by Jeanie Eberhardt of Layton,
New Jersey; 12" square, 13" high. (Photography by Richard
Brown & Assoc.)

Coil and dyed grapevine basket made by Jeanie Eberhardt
in Layton, New Jersey; 1983; 8" diameter, 6 1/2" high.
(Photograph, Richard Brown & Assoc.)

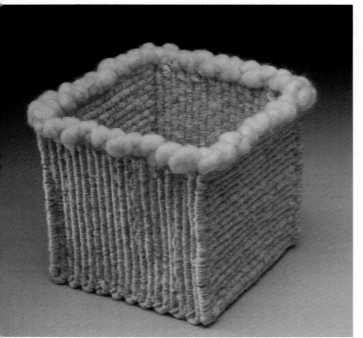

Coil Baskets

Dynamic modern coil baskets with decorations made in 1983 by Jane Niejadlik, Northampton, Massachusetts.

Three deep coil baskets ready for filling in the Pennsylvania Farm Museum.

Reed coil basket made by Maria Marta at Mission San Buenaventura, Ventura County, California in 1832; 16" diameter, 9 1/2" high. (National Gallery of Art)

Coil sewing basket with two firm bentwood handles attached to the sides, and an oak splint raised foot, probably from the Mechanicsburg area of Pennsylvania.

Coil storage basket made by native Indians at Lillout, British Columbia. (Photograph courtesy Museum of the American Indian, Heye Foundation)

Coil bee skep with oak splints and oak bottom rim.

Round coil storage basket suitable for honey and a coil bee skep with entrance cut into the fourth coil.

A group of coil baskets all made in Hanover, Pennsylvania; left, standing openwork round basket 11'' diameter, 4'' high; openwork basket with grapes, 12 1/4'' long, 8'' deep, 4'' high; standing basket with two handles, 12'' long, 9'' deep, 4 1/4'' high; openwork basket with apples, 12'' long, 8 1/2'' deep, 3'' high. (Eugene and Dorothy Elgin)

Two rye coil bee skeps; left, European wide coil skep with wooden plug at top and platform for landing bees, 19'' high; right, American with small slit entrance in the bottom coil and two crossing sticks to support the wax comb inside, 12'' high.

Three Pennsylvania coil openwork baskets; left, from Lewistown, 9" diameter, 3" high; center, from Dauphin County, 10" long, 7" deep, 3 1/2" high: right, from Newville, 9" diameter, 3" high. (Eugene and Dorothy Elgin)

Coil openwork basket with three varieties of splint weavers. At the center are cane weavers followed by two rows of weavers dyed green, and the remaining rows with oak splint weavers. This basket came from Biglersville, Pennsylvania. 9" diameter, 4" high. (Eugene and Dorothy Elgin)

Two coil openwork baskets on raised feet. Left, sewing basket from Annville, Lebanon County, Pennsylvania, with oak splints and raised oak foot; 11" diameter, 4" high. Right, sewing basket from Mechanicsburg, Pennsylvania, 12 1/2" diameter, 4 1/2" high. (Eugene and Dorothy Elgin)

Coil Baskets

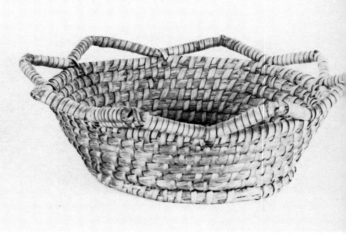

On this page and the following page are a group of coil openwork baskets with oak weavers made for sewing or other domestic work. All these originated in Pennsylvania.

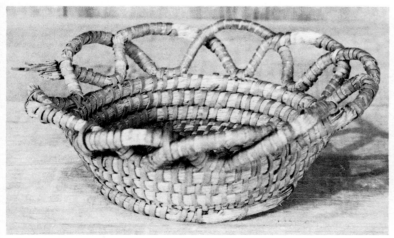

Rye straw and oak splint sewing basket from Pennsylvania
German origin in York County, Pennsylvania, 1800-1850,
13" long, 7" high. (Eugene and Dorothy Elgin)

Coil market basket with firm handle and raised foot from
Lenhartsville, Berks County, Pennsylvania; 19 1/2" long,
15" wide, 18" high.

Two coil market baskets with firm handle
which are secured in two different manner
Left, oval basket with handle pinned with
wooden plug to the sides (see detail). Rig
round basket with handle interwoven to t
sides. (Eugene and Dorothy Elgin)

Rye straw coil market basket with firm handle woven into the sides and reinforced by wrapped coils from near Lancaster, Pennsylvania. 15 1/2" diameter, 12 1/2" high.

Oval coil market basket with twisted vine handle; 9" long and 6" high. (Pennsylvania Farm Museum)

Coil basket with long bentwood handle, probably used to collect church offering; 12" diameter, 5 1/2" high, with 40" handle.

Two braided coil baskets formed as a market basket and a field basket.

Oval coil basket with oak weavers and one openwo handle.

Coil field basket with bentwood handles
interwoven at the sides (see detail).

Coil utility basket with 2 openwork handles on the sides.

Two miniature openwork coil baskets made by Southwest American Indians; left, 2 1/2" diameter; right, 2 1/4" diameter.

Grapevine and coil market basket made by Jeanie Eberhardt, of Layton, New Jersey, 13" diameter, 12" high. (Photograph by Richard Brown & Assoc.)

Hanging coil basket with one bentwood handle, 12" wide, 11" deep, 4 1/2" high.

Coil sewing basket with two firm bentwood handles, 19" diameter, 9 1/2" high.

Coil sewing basket with two firm bentwood handles and an original pincushion attached to the side. Made near Ephrata, Pennsylvania; 9" diameter, 4 1/4" high.

Left, oval coil basket with two wrapped openwork handles in the sides, from Uniontown, Maryland; 14 3/4" long, 5 1/2" deep, 4" high. Right, small oval market basket with oak splints and oak firm handle, from Pennsylvania; 11 1/2" long, 6 1/2" deep, 8" high. (Eugene and Dorothy Elgin)

Bibliography

Adovasio, J.M.

1970a The Origin and Development of Western Archaic Textiles and Basketry. *Tebiwa* 13(2): 1-40.

1970b Textiles. In Hogup Cave, by C.M. Aikens. *University of Utah Anthropoligical Papers* 93: 133-153.

1971 Some Comments on the Relationship of Great Basin Textiles to Textiles from the Southwest. *University of Oregon Anthropological Papers* 1: 103-108.

1974 Prehistoric North American Basketry. *Nevada State Museum Anthropological Papers* 16(5): 133-153.

1975a Prehistoric Great Basin Textiles. In *Irene Emery Roundtable on Museum Textiles 1974 Proceedings*, edited by P.L. Fiske, pp. 141-148. The Textile Museum, Washington, D.C.

1975b Fremont Basketry. *Tebiwa* 17(2): 67-76.

1976 Basketry from Swallow Shelter (42Bo268). In Swallow Shelter and Associated Sites, by G.F. Dalley. *University of Utah Anthopological Papers* 96: 167-169.

1977 *Basketry Technology*. Aldine Publishing Co., Chicago.

1980a Prehistoric Basketry of Western North America and Mexico. In *Early Native Americans: Prehistoric Demography, Economy and Technology*, edited by D.L. Browman, pp. 341-362. Mouton, The Hague.

1980b The Evolution of Basketry Manufacture in Northeastern Mexico, Lower and Trans-Pecos Texas. In Papers on the Prehistory of Northeastern Mexico and Adjacent Texas, edited by J.F. Epstein, T.R. Hester and C. Graves. *The University of Texas at San Antonio Center for Archaeological Research Special Report* 9: 93-102.

n.d. a Coahuila Coiled Basketry. In Contributions to Coahuila Prehistory, by W.W. Taylor, et al., edited by R.C. Carlisle and J.M. Adovasio. *Ethnology Monographs* (in press).

n.d. b Basketry. In *Handbook of North American Indians* (Vol. 16), *Technology and Visual Arts*, edited by W.C. Sturtevant. Smithsonian Institution, Washington, D.C. (in press).

n.d. c Prehistoric Great Basin Textiles. In *Handbook of North American Indians* (Vol. 10), *Great Basin*, edited by W. D'Azevedo. Smithsonian Institution, Washington, D.C. (in press).

n.d. d Netting. In *Handbook of North American Indians* (Vol. 16), *Technology and Visual Arts*, edited by W.C. Sturtevant. Smithsonian Institution, Washington, D.C. (inpress).

n.d. e Basketry from Moorehead Cave. In Moorehead Cave, by R.F. Maslowski. *Ethnology Monographs* (in press).

Adovasio, J.M. and R.L. Andrews

1980 Basketry and miscellaneous Perishable Artifacts from Walpi. In Textiles, Basketry and Shell Remains from Walpi, by K.P. Kent, J.M. Adovasio, R. Andrews, J.D. Nations and J.L. Adams. *Walpi Archaeological Project -Phase II* (Vol. 6), pp. 1-93. A Report Submitted to the Heritage, Conservation and Recreation Service, Interagency Archeological Services, San Francisco by the Museum of Northern Arizona.

1983 Material Culture of Gatecliff Shelter: Basketry, Cordage and Miscellaneous Fiber Constructions. In The Archaeology of Monitor Valley 2. Gatecliff Shelter, by D.H. Thomas. *Publications of the American Museum of Natural History* 59(1): 279-289.

1984 *The Origins of Perishable Production East of the Rockies*. A Paper Presented at the 49th Annual Meeting of the Society for American Archaeology, Portland, Oregon, April 1984.

n.d. Basketry from Baker Cave, by T. Hester (in press).

Adovasio, J.M., R.L. Andrews and R.C. Carlisle

1976 The Evolution of Basketry Manufacture in the Northern Great Basin. *Tebiwa* 18(2): 1-8.

1977 Perishable Industries from Dirty Shame Rockshelter. *Tebiwa Miscellaneous Papers of the Idaho State Museum*.7.

n.d. Perishable Industries from Dirty Shame Rockshelter. *University of Oregon Anthropological Papers* (in press).

Adovasio, J.M., R.L. Andrews (External Correlations prepared with R.C. Carlisle)

1980 Basketry, Cordage and Bark Impressions from the Northern Thorn Mound (46Mg78), Monongalia County, West Virginia. *West Virginia* 30: 33-72.

Adovasio, J.M., R.L. Andrews, R.C. Carlisle and R.D. Drennan

n.d. Fur Archaeological from Avayalik Island, Extreme Northern Labrador. In Avayalik Island, by R.H. Jordan and W. Fitzhugh. *Smithsonian Contributions to Anthropology* (in press).

Adovasio, J.M., R.C. Carlisle and R.L. Andrews

1978 An Evolution of Anasazi Basketry: A View from Antelope House. *New World Archaeology* 2(5): 1-5.

Adovasio, J.M. and J.D. Gunn

1975 Basketry and Basketmakers at Antelope House. *The Kiva* 41(1): 71-80.

1977 Style, Basketry and Basketmakers at Antelope House. In *The Individual in Prehistory: Studies of Variability in Style in Prehistoric Technologies*, edited by J.N. Hill and J. Gunn, pp. 137-153. Academic Press, New York.

Adovasio, J.M. and T.F. Lynch

1973 Preceramic Textiles from Guitarrero Cave, Peru. *American Antiquity* 38(1): 84-90.

Adovasio, J.M. and R.F. Maslowski

1980 Textiles and Cordage. In *Guitarrero Cave*, by T.F. Lynch, pp. 253-290. Academic Press, New York.

Adovasio, J.M., et al.

n.d. Basketry from Antelope House. In *Antelope House*, by D. Morris, et al. *Publications of the National Park Service* (in press).

American Indian Basketry: I-IV.

Andrews, R.L. and J.M. Adovasio

n.d. Knotted Cordage from Squaw Rockshelter, Aurora Run, Cuyahoga County, Ohio. In Squaw Rockshelter, by D. Brose. *Kirtlandia* (in press).

Andrews, R.L., J.M. Adovasio, R.C. Carlisle, G. Frison and R. Edgar

1984 A Prehistoric Net from Sheep Mountain, Wyoming: Analysis, Comparisons and Implications. Ms. on file, Department of Anthropology, University of Pittsburgh.

Bay View 15.

Bedwell, S.F.

1973 *Fort Rock Basin Prehistory and Environment*. University of Oregon Books, Eugene.

Bobart, H.H. *Basketwork through the Ages*, Geoffrey Cumberlege, Oxford University Press, London, 1936.

Carpentier, D. and J. Bachelet

1982 *Basketry*. E.P. Publishing, Ltd., Wakefield, West Yorkshire, England.

Chapman, J. and J.M. Adovasio

1977 Textile and Basketry Impressions from Icehouse Bottom, Tennessee. *American Antiquity* 42(4): 620-625. Cressman, L.D. et al.

1942 Archaeological Researches in the Northern Great Basin. *Carnegie Institution of Washington Publication* 538.

Dockstader, F.J.

1973 *Indian Art of the Americas*, Museum of the American Indian, Heye Foundation, New York.

Driver, H.E.

1961 *Indians of North America*. University of Chicago Press, Chicago.

Gould, M.E.

1962 Early American Splint Work. *The Antiques Journal*, June: 14-15.

Hart, C. and D.

1976 *Natural Basketry*. Watson-Guptill Publications, New York.

Hopf. C.

1965 Basketware of the Northeast. A Survey of the types of Basketware used on the Farm from the Colonial Period to 1860. Cooperstown Graduation Program, Cooperstown, New York.

Irwin, J.R.

1982 *Baskets and Basket Makers in Southern Appalachia*, Schiffer Publishing, Exton, Pennsylvania.

James, G.W.

1903 *Indian Basketry* (3rd edition). G.W. James, Pasadena, California.

Ketchum, W.C., Jr.

1974 *American Basketry and Woodenware*. MacMillan Publishing Company, Inc., New York.

Klippel, W.E.

1971 Graham Cave Revisited: A Re-evaluation of its Cultural Position During the Archaic Period. *Missouri State Archaeological Society Memoir* 9.

Knapp, E.S.

1901 *Raphia and Reed Weaving*. Milton Bradley Co., Springfield, Massachusetts.

Lamb, F.W.

1972 *Indian Baskets of North America*. Riverside Museum Press, Riverside, California.

Larason, L.

1978 *The Basket Collectors Book*. Scorpio Publications, Chal font, Pennsylvania.

Lasansky, J.

1979 *Willow, Oak & Rye, Basket Traditions in Pennsylvania*. Pennsylvania State University Press, University Park, Pennsylvania.

Logan, W.D.

1952 Graham Cave: An Archaic Site in Montgomery County, Missouri. *Missouri Archaeological Society Memoir* 2.

Mason, O.T.

1904 Aboriginal American Basketry: Studies in a Textile Art Without Machinery. *Report of the U.S. National Museum for 1902*, pp. 171-548.

Poese, W.

1971 A Tisket, a Tasket. *Antiques Journal*, October: 16, 17, 28.

Raycraft, D. and C.

1976 *Country Baskets*. Wallace-Homestead Book Company, Des Moines, Iowa.

Roosevelt, A.C. and J.G.E. Smith, eds.

1979 *The Ancestors, Native Artisans of the Americas*. Museum of the American Indian, New York.

Rose, M.C. and E.M., eds.

1977 *A Shaker Reader*. Universe Books, New York.

Seeler, K. and E.

1972 *Nantucket Lightship Baskets*. The Deermouse Press, Nantucket, Massachusetts.

Stephenson, S.H.

1977 *Basketry of the Appalachian Mountains*. Van Norstrand.

Stile, T.E.

1982 Perishable Artifacts from Meadowcroft Rockshelter, Washington County, Southwestern Pennsylvania. In *Meadowcroft: Collected Papers on the Archaeology of Meadowcroft Rockshelter and the Cross Creek Drainage*, edited by R.C. Carlisle and J.M. Adovasio, pp. 130-141. Department of Anthropology, University of Pittsburgh, Pittsburgh. Teleki, G.R.

1975 *The Baskets of Rural America*. E.P. Dutton, New York.

1979 *Collecting Traditional American Basketry*. E.P. Dutton, New York.

Vlach, J.M.

1978 *The Afro-American Tradition in Decorative Arts*. The Cleveland Museum of Art, Cleveland.

Weltfish, G.

1930 Prehistoric North American Basketry Techniques and Modern Distributions. *American Anthropologist* 32: 454-495.

Index